Living in a Body
with a
Mind of its Own

Living in a Body with a Mind of its Own

The Emotional Journey of Dystonia

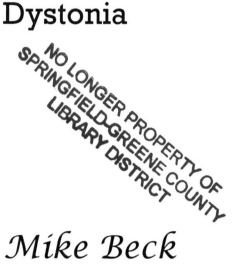
Rev. Mike Beck

authorHOUSE®

AuthorHouse™ LLC
1663 Liberty Drive
Bloomington, IN 47403
www.authorhouse.com
Phone: 1-800-839-8640

Published by AuthorHouse   07/05/2013

ISBN: 978-1-4817-6508-4 (sc)
ISBN: 978-1-4817-6507-7 (hc)
ISBN: 978-1-4817-6506-0 (e)

Library of Congress Control Number: 2013910839

Any people depicted in stock imagery provided by Thinkstock are models, and such images are being used for illustrative purposes only.

Certain stock imagery © Thinkstock.

This book is printed on acid-free paper.

Because of the dynamic nature of the Internet, any web addresses or links contained in this book may have changed since publication and may no longer be valid. The views expressed in this work are solely those of the author and do not necessarily reflect the views of the publisher, and the publisher hereby disclaims any responsibility for them.

Contents

Appendix

Nothing surpasses the holiness of those who

have learned perfect acceptance of everything that is.

In the game of cards called life one plays

the hand one is dealt to the best of one's ability.

Those who insist on playing, not the hand they have been

given, but the one they insist they should have been dealt;

these are life's failures.

We are not asked if we will play.

That is not an option.

Play we must. The option is how.

From *Taking Flight*, by Anthony de Mello

Dedication

This book is dedicated to my wife, Mickey. When we married in 1970, little did you realize how much you would live out the promise that you would be there for me "in sickness and in health."

Mickey battles her own illnesses, suffering from severe fibromyalgia along with a degenerative bone condition. Yet in the midst of her own pain, she has always been there to help not only me, but also her family and hundreds of other people in the churches we have served.

She has been with me every step of this tiresome journey, patiently sitting in countless waiting rooms as I went through 11 surgeries and hundreds of visits to doctors for botox injections.

Since the onset of blepharospasm in 2004, she has been my chauffer 98 percent of the time. She says she can put the car on remote control to make the 600-mile round-trip from Indianapolis to Nashville and back!

She has put up with my depression as well as my fear and anxiety related to an uncertain future. She has shared with me numerous disappointments when surgeries did not provide the results we had so desperately hoped for.

Along with me and countless other persons, she has asked God "why" a productive ministry had to be cut short in the prime of my career. Like everyone who deals with adversity, those questions remain unanswered on this side of eternity. She and I have simply had to put our trust in God, knowing that the Scriptures reveal God's grace and strength are sufficient for each new day.

She, along with my two sons, their wonderful wives, and my four precious grandchildren have provided the words of encouragement and perspective when I had neither the strength or will to continue on.

Not even Mickey, as close as she is to me, can ever fully understand what it is like to live with dystonia. Only those who have lived with its never-ending negative effects can understand what it is like to walk this ever uncertain road.

You never expected these things which are now a reality for us when you said "I do" over 40 years ago. But for the beautiful, precious person that you are, this book is dedicated to you. I thank you for being willing to travel this lonely road with me. Together, we have learned that the cup of life is always at least half-full. I love you with all my heart.

About the Author

Rev. Mike Beck holds degrees from Taylor University, Butler University, and Asbury Theological Seminary. After spending ten years as a teacher, coach, and school administrator, Mike felt the call to pastoral ministry. For the next 22 years, he served churches in Greensburg, Corydon, and Franklin, Indiana before going on disability in 2006.

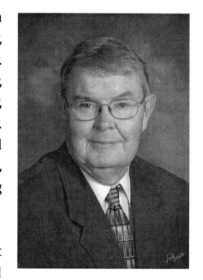

This is his second book. His first book was published in 2011 and titled, ***No Longer Silent: Doing Pastoral Ministry With Excellence and Grace.*** Mike currently suffers from four dystonias, and his concern for people who battle with this rare, neurological illness has led to the writing of this second book.

Rev. Mike and his wife, Mickey, have been married for over 40 years. They have two sons and four grandchildren. His hobbies are golf and travel.

For more information related to dystonia or to schedule Mike and Mickey for a speaking engagement, e-mail him at revmikebeck@comcast.net

Acknowledgments

I want to thank the gifted professional staff at the Vanderbilt Voice Center, especially Dr. Catherine Garrett, Dr. James Netterville, Dr. Mark Corey, and the many speech therapists who have worked with me for the past 20 years. You are simply the best!

I want to thank Dr. Sara Schrader who was instrumental in getting me an appointment at the Mayo Clinic in Scottsdale, Arizona, and to Dr. Virgil Evidente who supervised my care while I underwent Deep Brain Stimulation surgery. I also thank Renee' and Carla, the nurses who have made adjustments to my "brain pacemakers" that have resulted in significant improvement.

I want to thank Dr. William Nunery, an outstanding eye surgeon, whose expertise has helped my blepharospasm to become more manageable.

I want to thank Dr. Allison Brashear and Dr. Matthew Bain who have given me injections of botox to treat my writer's cramp. You have not only allowed me to write again, but you have improved my golf score by nearly five strokes!

I want to thank the people of Old Capitol, Franklin Grace, and Dearborn Hills United Methodist churches whose love, caring, and support have carried me and taught me so much about God's work of grace over the past 20 years.

I want to thank Sharon Rothrock, a retired English teacher, who helped in the editing of this book.

I want to thank those individuals whose financial gifts helped to underwrite the initial publishing costs of this book.

I want to thank Karen Miller for her assistance with the photograph and design of the cover. Karen creates beautiful cards with her original photography. For more information, e-mail her at bkmiller52@comcast.net.

And finally, I want to extend my sincere thanks to my family and many friends who have been there for me in so many different ways over these past 21 years. You will never know how much it has meant to me.

Endorsements

In this wonderfully written book by Rev. Mike Beck, he has helped to illuminate the challenges of life with dystonia. Throughout the book, Rev. Beck's sense of humor, courage, as well as moments of reflection shine through. His willingness to let God use "the dark strands of life" along with the "gold and silver" in weaving the tapestry of his life give credence to his optimism even when being forced to live with four different dystonias.

This is must reading for those battling any form of chronic illness, not just dystonia. It should also be required reading for those person's families, friends, and care givers in order to understand more clearly the daily struggles and emotional ups and downs of those faced with chronic illness.

It has been my privilege observing and helping with the medical care of this man who has displayed such grace and dignity under life's difficult trials.

*Dr. **William Nunery** is a Doctor of Ophthalmology, specializing in oculofacial plastic and orbital surgery. Dr. Nunery is a highly respected eye surgeon whose expertise is known throughout the country. He is the physician responsible for treating Rev. Mike's blepharospasm.*

Rev. Mike Beck has spent the past twenty years "living in a body with a mind of its own." Instead of allowing his dystonias to limit his outreach, Mike has courageously and purposefully allowed this neurological disorder to serve as a foundation for his own spiritual growth as well as linking arms with others who struggle with the emotions that are a part of this rare disorder.

In this book, Rev. Mike has "found his voice" once again, sharing soul-stirring encouragement to others who suffer from dystonia as well as offering practical insights to any reader dealing with adversity in their own lives.

***Elaine Olsen** is a Christian author and speaker. A cancer survivor, she has authored two books, "Peace For the Journey" and "Beyond Cancer's Scars." For more information about her books, log onto her website at www. peaceforthejourney.com*

Rev. Mike Beck was the first person I met who understood my diagnosis of cervical dystonia. When he learned of my medical condition, he immediately reached out to help in my struggle. Mike has four dystonias to wrestle with on a daily basis, so I consider him something of an expert on this illness.

Mike's book explains medical information on botox along with oral medications and surgical options. He has added touches of humor to lighten the tone of a very serious subject. I especially enjoyed his section on the emotions felt by those who have this disorder. As he so truthfully stated, we will deal with our afflicted body for the remainder of our lives.

He then goes further to help us spiritually deal with dystonia-related problems. Without God's grace, I could not have handled the journey through medical treatment and on to accepting my disorder as a way of life. God still has a plan for us if we will allow Him to lead us down life's path.

I thank Mike for sharing his gift of writing. I have learned, laughed, cried, and healed spiritually while reading this book. His book is a reminder that none of us need to feel alone in our daily battle with dystonia.

Sandy Blackwell *was the former Administrative Assistant to the South Indiana Conference before being affected by cervical dystonia which forced her to resign and go on disability.*

Foreword

In my research on dystonia, I have discovered many books written from a medical perspective. Some of these have been very helpful in understanding the disease that forces me to "live in a body with a mind of its own."

However, I have found few books that deal with the emotional aspects of living with this very misunderstood illness. I have written this book in the hope that it will be helpful to others who suffer from this awful condition.

My guess is you also suffer from dystonia or know someone who does. I trust, through the vulnerability of which I have tried to write, you will better understand the often unspoken emotions pent-up within a person suffering from this currently incurable illness.

I have chosen to write in the first-person, discussing the four dystonias that afflict me: spasmodic dysphonia, blepharospasm, meige's syndrome, and writer's cramp. My hope is that through my story, although your situation may be different than mine, you will discover many of the same feelings resonating within yourself. Discovering that what you are feeling is "normal" is usually a very liberating experience.

These past twenty years have been very difficult for me, but it has also been a time for reflection and learning to more effectively deal with my affliction. The book can also provide insights and be of help to people in their struggle with any of life's adversities.

I hope those who take time to read this book will realize, although there are ways a person suffering from dystonia learns to cope and adjust to this illness, it is a far more devastating disorder than most people are willing to acknowledge, especially from the emotional aspects involved.

Living in a body which does things that are beyond our control is a very difficult experience. None of us want pity. However, we do want people around us to realize that every day is a struggle for us, and we would simply like this strange illness to be acknowledged and better understood.

Therefore, I invite you to join me on a road that none of us afflicted by this illness ever expected to travel; a road that is often invisible to others around us; and a road with strange twists and turns along the way. It's a road that never ends in this life, but for those who are afflicted by dystonia, I hope your reading this book results in the road being a little easier to travel. I welcome you as we learn more about the personal emotions experienced by people suffering from dystonia.

PART 1

My Journey with Dystonia

A Life Filled With Blessings

Lou Gehrig, nicknamed the "Iron Horse," played 1st base for the New York Yankees in the 1920's and 1930's. At his retirement ceremony, he uttered these famous words: "Today I consider myself to be the luckiest man on the face of the earth." At the time, he was battling ALS Syndrome which would come to be known as "Lou Gehrig's Disease."

Now in no way would I compare myself with Lou Gehrig, in stature or in the severity of his illness. However, there is a sense in which the two illnesses are somewhat related. Individuals battling ALS over time lose muscle function, and as the disease worsens, they eventually lose the ability to breathe, resulting in their death.

With dystonia, people find certain muscles being over-active, causing them to twist and spasm in strange kinds of ways. Unlike ALS, dystonia rarely results in death. However, there is extreme frustration, difficulty in performing certain actions, and with some dystonias, chronic pain.

I must begin by acknowledging that my life has been filled with numerous blessings. For the first 16 years of my life, I lived on a farm. I didn't particularly enjoy farm life, but looking back there were so many wonderful experiences my three siblings and I enjoyed which could have been found in no other environment.

I was blessed with two God-fearing parents who shared love and modeled a strong faith to me, my older sister, and my two younger brothers. My Dad died in 2010, but as of the writing of this book, I am fortunate to have my Mom still with me.

I went to college at Taylor University where my faith matured and became stronger, primarily due to two men. One was Don Odle who was my golf coach for two years and one of the outstanding small college basketball coaches of his era. The other man was Bob Davenport, a two-time All-American fullback in the1950's, who was the football coach at Taylor and directed a summer bicycling program known as the Wandering Wheels.

I had the privilege of working for Bob and traveled with him and 40 other college guys in 1968 on a six-week, 4,000 mile bike trip from the Golden Gate Bridge in San Francisco to the Statue of Liberty in New York. It was indeed an experience of a lifetime.

The cycling continued for the next nine years with the establishment of my own group known as "The Spokesmen." From 1969 until 1977, myself and the three members of my staff had the privilege of influencing over 1,000 junior and senior high youth on 15 major trips throughout the United States, England, and Europe along with numerous week-end bike trips.

I married my high school sweetheart just before my senior year in college. I had ten wonderful years in education as a teacher, coach, and school administrator. It was during those years that God blessed us with two sons, Aaron and Adam. They would grow up and marry two wonderful wives, who we think of as the daughters we never had.

It was during the latter part of my years in education when I felt God's call to pastoral ministry. We had three great years at

Asbury Seminary in Kentucky. There I was blessed to learn under outstanding professors and made life-long friends.

My first pastorate was in Greensburg, Indiana where I served as the Associate Pastor for five years. The people there loved and nurtured our family, and it was during those years that I had the privilege to take the first of three trips to Israel.

Our next pastorate was at Old Capitol United Methodist Church in Corydon where I was the senior pastor of a dynamic congregation. They provided us with a beautiful parsonage to live in, and it was there that both boys finished high school. We completed a major addition and remodeling project at the church, and it was during my time in Corydon that I made the first of two mission trips to Africa, experiences that changed my life and caused me to realize how fortunate I was. Six people entered into full-time ministry during my eight years in Corydon. It was at Old Capitol where my battle with spasmodic dysphonia began in 1992.

I moved on to serve Franklin Grace UMC from 1997-2006. Despite my struggle with speaking, the church grew by 50 percent, and we built a large and beautiful two-story wing devoted to children and youth ministries. While serving in Franklin, I received a major grant from the Eli Lilly Foundation to take a three-month, once-in-a-lifetime trip through the western United States and to England to tour historical sites related to the founder of Methodism, John Wesley.

The people at Grace were wonderful to us, but during my last two years there I developed blepharospasm and meige's syndrome, two more dystonias affecting my eyes and the muscles in my lower face. The writer's cramp also became more severe. In 2006, the combined effect of battling four dystonias forced me to ask my Bishop for a medical disability leave.

While pastoring at Grace, I met a young woman who was studying at the Indiana University School of Medicine. I officiated at her wedding to the grandson of one of my members. While in Phoenix a couple of years later, over dinner one evening with Sara and her husband, I learned she was doing an internship at the Mayo Clinic in Scottsdale.

It was her assistance that enabled me to quickly get into the Mayo Clinic there *(I had spoken with the Mayo Clinic in Jacksonville, Florida, only to find the soonest I could get an appointment was in 18 months!).* When I returned to Phoenix in November of 2005, they determined I would be a good candidate for Deep Brain Stimulation surgery, a surgery they were beginning to do on patients suffering from multiple dystonias.

During my eight years at Grace, I was also fortunate to become good friends with the wife of a retired Bishop in the United Methodist Church. She provided the funds to cover the medical costs not covered by my insurance along with helping out with my expenses during the month I spent at Mayo for DBS Surgery. I will be forever grateful for her kindness.

I tried to return to ministry about a year after the DBS surgery, serving part-time at Dearborn Hills UMC. The people there showered us with love despite my disabilities and helped me to learn that "I was not my illness," a lesson I find myself continually needing to re-learn.

However, with the four dystonias, even this limited ministry proved too much for me to handle, and we had to leave the church in 2010. God once again provided for our needs, helping us to locate a lovely, three-bedroom home at a price we could afford in Mooresville, Indiana.

I have often remarked at funeral services that there are ultimately three things in life that truly matter: family, faith, and friends. I have been extremely blessed with all three of these things given to me in abundance by a God who uses even our weaknesses for His glory. I don't like living with my dystonias, but I can honestly say that I have been richly blessed. Like Lou Gehrig, I can say today, "I am among the luckiest men on the face of the earth."

The Onset of Spasmodic Dysphonia

It was a warm Sunday morning in the spring of 1992. My parents were visiting our family in Corydon and attended the morning worship service. The sermon was well-received and my congregation was attentive, but I noticed I had great difficulty in getting out my words. My voice had been somewhat "shaky" at times during the past several years, but I attributed this simply to nerves.

Following lunch, my Dad and I were sitting at the kitchen table. I said to him, "Dad, I'm really scared. My speaking is getting worse every day." To a preacher, one's voice is how he or she makes a living.

By the following Sunday, during the early part of the service, I could only get out about two of every five words, and what speech I had was very strained and required great effort on my part. I asked my associate pastor to read my sermon that day and the following three Sundays while I searched for answers to the problem.

I went to an E.N.T. Doctor who did a throat exam and tested me for allergies. After about three weeks had passed, a lady in my congregation came to me and said, "Rev. Mike, you sound just like my husband did before he went for an experimental treatment at John's Hopkins Medical Center. Their family were among the first people I had ministry with upon arriving at Old Capitol. The way his voice sounded, without any answers as to "why" this was taking place, caused him to simply take off driving before returning home a couple of days later.

His wife gave me material to read about spasmodic dysphonia. I remember driving on the interstate in Louisville on the way to making a hospital call as Mickey read the indicators of S.D. *(spasmodic dysphonia)*. To each indicator, my answer was: "Yes, that's true of my condition."

I ask you, what are the odds of a member of my congregation of 300 having the same rare illness as I did, an illness that affects less than ½ percent of the entire population! When I went back to the doctor the next week, I said to him, "I think I know what's going on. I think I may have spasmodic dysphonia." The doctor agreed and scheduled an appointment for me at the Vanderbilt Voice Center in Nashville, Tennessee.

When I arrived in Nashville, the doctors at the Voice Center confirmed the diagnosis of S.D. They explained that currently there was no cure, but that injections of botulinum toxin into the small muscles that controlled the vocal chords would give me relief for a period of time. They said I was fortunate to have received a quick diagnosis.

They told me that the average patient spent more than two years going from doctor to doctor trying to find out what was wrong. This illness was not well known in the field of medicine, and thus they received numerous incorrect diagnoses. In the end, many folks were told that the problem was simply "in their head," and they were prescribed various psychotic medications. They told me of one lady who would literally shut herself in a closet at times because she could not speak in a way that others could understand!

They set the date of my first botox injection for the following day. Ironically, it was our 22nd wedding anniversary.

Botox:
The Poison That Helps

I distinctly remember going for my first botox injection. Surely being injected in the throat was something that would be painful. The nurses were pleasant and called me back into a room where they attached the end of two wires to my neck and forehead, leaving the wires dangling around my neck.

Then they moved me to another room where I waited until it was time for my injection. It was comforting to see the hallways lined with gold records autographed by country music stars who had been to the Voice Center for treatment of a variety of voice problems. Ironically, a man walked by the room where I was waiting. Dressed totally in black, he stuck his head in the door and said "good morning" and then moved on. I turned to my wife and said, "That was Johnny Cash!"

Finally they came and got me. As they were walking me to the treatment room, I wondered if this was what it felt like when being escorted to the electric chair! When I arrived at the treatment room, they connected one wire to the syringe that held the botox and the other wire to a device that recorded the sound of muscle activity.

After discussing what dosage to put into the muscles on both sides *(a unit represents the amount of botox that would kill one laboratory mouse),* they decided on 2.5 units per side, a rather standard option for a first treatment. The doctor injected some numbing medication and then inserted the 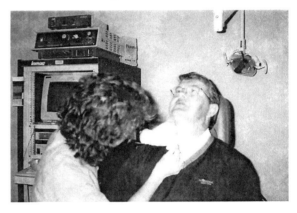 needle containing the botox. After about three minutes, the doctor felt the needle was in the correct muscle and asked me to hold out an "eee" sound. I could hear a distinct crackling sound of increased intensity coming from the device that recorded muscle activity. The botox was injected, and we moved on to the muscle controlling the other vocal chord. The entire process took only about fifteen minutes with hardly any discomfort. I was given a form to evaluate four qualities related to my voice on a weekly basis, and then I was on my way home.

Over the next 20 years, botox and I would become very good friends. I came to realize that it was a treatment, not a cure. In simple terms, botox works by creating a barrier between the muscle and the nerve endings for a period of time. This barrier prevents the impulse coming from the nerve to the muscle telling it to respond from being able to get through. Most people have a very weak voice for about three weeks; then the voice becomes relatively normal for about six weeks; and then the strain and effort to speak returns.

At that point, it is time to return for another injection. In one sense, it is similar to riding a roller coaster. At first you go up a long hill *(the weak and breathy stage),* then you experience the thrill of the ride *(the time when the voice is fairly normal),* and then the coaster slows down and returns to its original starting point *(analogous to the return of the strained voice I had at the beginning).* I have ridden this roller coaster over 100 times during the past 20 years.

I used to believe college professors who worked in research were wasting their time. I believed they should be in the classroom teaching students. But who would believe a toxic poison could be used to help treat a currently incurable disease! I now better appreciate those devoted scientists, who through trial and error, help us find treatments and develop new medications to fight a variety of illnesses.

I was ecstatic when I returned home. I had a voice once again, free from the strain and effort I had originally experienced. Before going to Vanderbilt, my doctor had asked if I would work with a speech therapist for a few weeks. I felt foolish in her office as she asked me to read children's books, even though I had great difficulty in getting out the words. Before my first botox shot, I was convinced she believed my problem was all psychological in nature.

When I went back to see her three weeks following my injection, I walked into her office and said, in a clear and strong voice: "Pam, what would you like to talk about today?" Her jaw dropped as she was shocked at the improvement in my voice, and she immediately reached for her tape recorder to make a recording. She was one of thousands of trained professionals in the field of medicine who had never heard of spasmodic dysphonia.

I returned to preaching, but we soon discovered that in my case the botox would last only about six weeks before the strained and effortful voice would return with a vengeance. After about three years of this, in consultation with my doctor, we decided to do a nerve avulsion surgery to paralyze one of the vocal chords. This would leave us with only one "monster" to deal with after the surgery instead of two!

Following the surgery, if the paralyzed chord ended up too far from a midline position, there would be a space between the two vocal chords when I spoke and my speech would be too weak and breathy. If it ended up past a center position, the two vocal chords would bang together resulting in a strained and effortful voice. Dr. Netterville explained it this way: the surgery was kind of like trying to balance on a thin wire fence. Two subsequent medialization surgeries were required to get the paralyzed vocal chord into a proper midline position.

However, with botox and the follow-up surgeries, combined with the help of my oldest son, a sound engineer who helped me find the best headset microphone available, I was able to stay in ministry for almost 20 more years.

Due to my voice limitations, I was now forced to learn a more Biblical way of doing ministry through empowering the laity for their ministry. There was a quote that I would often use with my congregation. I would tell them, "I may not be able to play my instrument as well as before, but I can still conduct the orchestra! And an orchestra makes far more beautiful music than a soloist."

It may not always be perfect, but I had a voice once again thanks to the skilled doctors and nurses at Vanderbilt and a poison named botox—"a poison that helps!"

Medicine is an Art,
Not a Science

One of the important lessons I learned from my many years of battling dystonia is this: "Medicine is an <u>art;</u> not a <u>science</u>."

Doctors are gifted human beings, filled with knowledge from many years of rigorous training. But we must recognize they are fallible human beings just like us, they do not have all the answers, and at times they make errors in judgment.

When I went for my first botox shot for spasmodic dysphonia, I felt we could find exactly the right dosage and thus would be able to accurately predict just how long we would need before the next injection. I was wrong. Over time, I realized the doctor was "going in blind" and could not be totally positive the needle was in the correct muscle. The doctor had to rely on the device which recorded the muscle activity. The muscles that control the vocal chords are very small, and errors in injecting the toxin sometimes take place. Also, the place in the muscle where the needle ends up can make a huge difference in the result.

As I mentioned earlier, we were unable to make my injections last more than five or six weeks during the first three years, while most people would get three to four months between injections.

With the expense of driving back and forth to Nashville so frequently, I realized we had to try something different.

I had done some research on the internet about nerve avulsion surgery as a treatment for spasmodic dysphonia. Dr. Netterville agreed that this surgery, in which he would take out the nerve to the muscle which controlled one vocal chord, might help in my case. However, he was careful to remind me that what we were doing would permanently paralyze one of my vocal chords, and so he left the final decision to me. I also learned one should take the decision to have surgery very seriously, as there can be adverse effects years later that you had not anticipated.

The decision was the right one, at least for the time being, as we were able to get the injections to last for three months. My ministry was able to continue with a voice much better than before.

However, ten years later things were not working as well as they had previously, and I scheduled another appointment with Dr. Netterville, who had since left the field of doing botox injections and was focusing entirely on laryngeal surgeries. He is the only doctor I have ever experienced who has lazy-boy chairs in his waiting room! The wait to see him can last as long as three hours, but people do not complain, as he takes whatever time is necessary to truly listen to and care for each patient. On this visit, he suggested that I consider trying an experimental surgery in which we would replace some of the vocal chord muscle with fat tissue, causing a softer "hit" when the vocal chords came together.

This helped for a time, but the end result was a large amount of scar tissue built up as a result of the four surgeries. At Vanderbilt, I heard resident students told on numerous occasions: "Rev. Beck's condition is unusual and more severe than most of our patients." On those occasions, I wished I was not so special!

As things got worse again, I had stopped by the desk at Dr. Netterville's office, hoping to schedule another appointment. I remember him coming over to Dr. Garrett's office where he said to me, with sincere sadness in his voice: "I'm sorry the things we have tried did not work out as we had hoped." Rarely do you find a physician willing to say this to a patient.

A couple of visits later, I asked Dr. Garrett if I could have another "scope" of my vocal chords. Upon her examining the results, I had to hear the words no patient ever wants to hear as she said to me: "Mike, I'm sorry, but there is nothing more we can do. The nerves have regenerated and connected in ways we don't understand. There is nothing else we can try except to continue the injections, perhaps less frequently than before, and hope for the best."

It was hard to hear those words. One always hopes that there is a "magic bullet" out there somewhere that will make everything right. But the lesson I have learned is physicians are human beings just like us. They do the very best they can with the information before them.

However, I have learned the reason for the phrase "the practice of medicine." The cold reality is there are not always solutions to our medical problems. Doctors do not have any "crystal ball" into which they can gaze to tell them exactly what to do. The reason is simple but sometimes hard to accept: "Medicine is indeed an art and not a science."

The Frustration of Writer's Cramp

Writer's cramp is perhaps the least serious of the four dystonias I deal with, and yet it has been just as frustrating as the other three. I had been told since my earliest years in school that I held a pen in a rather unique way. But it felt natural to me, and the quality of my writing, especially my printing, was outstanding.

The onset of this dystonia happened about the same time as my struggle with spasmodic dysphonia. Because speaking was much more essential to my profession than writing, I placed this problem on the "back burner." I was an excellent typist, and the use of my computer could substitute for most of my need to write.

However, with the passing of time, writing became more and more difficult. I would do anything possible to avoid having other people see me write. When forced to write, my hand would shake as if I had Parkinson's disease. It was both frustrating and embarrassing.

The ironic thing was the hand was fully functional when engaging in most other activities. I could write on a chalk board, use scissors, or hold a baseball bat or golf club with no problems. It was only when I held a pen to write that the problem would manifest itself.

I consulted with Dr. Alison Brasher at the I.U. Medical Center to see if there was any help available for this condition. She indicated this problem might be corrected by injections of botox. She asked if I wanted to give this option a try, and my immediate answer was "yes."

The muscles that control writing are not located in the hand but in the lower part of the forearm. She would ask me to move my third and fourth fingers until she felt she had located 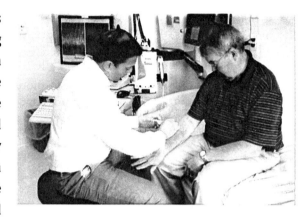 the correct muscle, and then she would inject the botox. She injected botox in about four different locations with no discomfort involved.

I was amazed at the results. After about a week, I noticed my third and fourth fingers were much lower than the other fingers of my right hand. There was no way that I could raise them up to their normal position. However, I could hold a pen again and write with the same degree of neatness I had exhibited many years ago. The only side-effects were that I needed to be careful when holding a cup in my right hand, and I sometimes had difficulty buttoning my shirts. But, unlike other dystonias where the injections would last two or three months, this injection was needed only twice a year to keep the dystonia under control.

On about the third injection for my writer's cramp, I asked her an unusual question. I told her that since receiving the injections, my golf score was almost five shots lower than before. I asked her if there was any connection between the botox and the improvement in my golf scores.

Dr. Brashear said she had heard this several times before from golfers she was treating for writer's cramp and asked if I played golf right-handed. Anyone who has played golf knows right-handed golfers should grip the club predominately with their left hand. The right-hand grip should be only about 50 percent as strong as the left-hand grip.

Injecting the right hand was forcing it to be weaker than the left hand, resulting in an improvement in my golf game! Dr. Brashear said she had a few patients, obviously with money in their pockets to burn, who would get injections for the sole purpose of improving their golf score!

Eventually Dr. Brashear would move on to take a position in research in North Carolina, and I began to be treated for writer's cramp by Dr. Matthew Bain. We have developed  a close relationship and the improvement has continued. I only wish the other dystonias responded as well to botox as the writer's cramp. However, my golf game has continued to improve as an added surprise!

Blepharospasm:
I Never Saw it Coming

I was playing golf with a good friend from Greensburg. On the 8th hole he had a 50-foot putt and asked me to tend the pin. For non-golfers, that is when you hold the flagstick until the other player putts so they can better see the location of the hole. As soon as they putt, you quickly remove the flagstick and move away from the hole.

Jim made a great putt that went in the hole, but I never removed the flagstick. Jim, knowing I knew the rules of golf well, asked, "Mike, what happened?" My simple reply was: "Jim, I never saw it coming." My eyes had shut at about the same time Jim putted, and I could not get them back open until his putt had reached the hole!

Such is the nature of blepharospasm. With no warning, the eyes close and one has to work very hard to get them re-opened. On other occasions, the eyes are constantly "twitching."

The incident described was of minor concern. However, when crossing a busy street, walking in a crowd, or trying to drive, blepharospasm is a very serious problem.

The blepaharospasm first appeared the day after my fourth laryngeal surgery where the surgeon had replaced some of the muscle in my vocal chord with fatty tissue. My wife came into my hospital room the next morning and almost immediately asked what was wrong with my eyes. They were twitching uncontrollably. Dr. Netterville explained there should have been no connection between the surgery and the onset of blepharospasm, but this is one of the unanswerable questions one learns to live with when afflicted by dystonia.

A few weeks later, I went back to Dr. Brashear. She referred me to an eye doctor at the Indiana Eye Institute. He concurred that I had an extreme case of blepharospasm and injected the muscles around the eye lids with botox. There was no improvement. I returned for a follow-up injection, and the dosage was increased to a very high level of 250 units, again without success.

The doctor referred me to Dr. William Nunery, an outstanding eye surgeon. He suggested we try four orbeculectomy surgeries over a month-long period of time. During these surgeries, Dr. Nunery removed some of the muscle in the upper and lower eyelids. He said in most cases this would take care of the blepharospasm.

The surgeries helped, but the problem remained, requiring further injections of botox. However, now the botox began to help to some degree. An even greater improvement 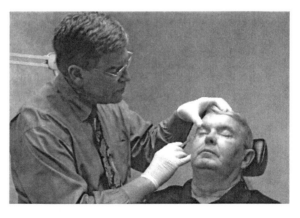 occurred following my Deep Brain Stimulation surgery. Dr. Nunery normally has a medical intern observing him, and again I would often hear the phrase, "Rev. Beck's case is more severe than most." Like what I often hear at Vanderbilt, in this case I'm rather tired of feeling special!

I was forced to give up driving except for short distances. This was a hard thing to do, as normally in married relationships it is the man who does most of the driving. In fact, today my wife was out-of-town and I had to make a 20-mile drive to Franklin to attend a family dinner. Due to the low level of the sun staring me in the eyes, I had to work very hard to keep my eyes open and focused on the road during this short trip.

Bright light is very hard on a person suffering from this dystonia, and I am forced to wear high intensity sunglasses. Working at the computer for extended periods of time is difficult. I still play a decent game of golf, but I often need to ask my playing companions where my ball ended up. My fear is someday I will make a hole-in-one and not have the joy of seeing the ball go into the hole!

One additional problem has developed in the past two years. Due to the four eye surgeries, combined with frequent botox injections, my eyes will not completely close. This results in a constant problem where my eyes become much too dry. This is a major irritation, and additional surgery may be needed later this year to correct this problem.

In a later chapter, I will discuss my Deep Brain Stimulation surgery. The blepharospasm and meige's syndrome have been helped the most as a result of this surgery. I am now able to keep my blepharospasm fairly well under control by injections of botox involving about 25 shots around each eye every 12 to 14 weeks.

Unlike my other botox injections, there is a reasonable amount of pain associated with these injections due to the sensitive tissue around the eyes. My normal dosage is 75 units around the perimeter of each eye. We are able to minimize the pain involved by putting on a numbing cream about 30 minutes prior to the injections, followed by the application of "Pain Ease," an extremely cold numbing spray that Dr. Nunery applies just before beginning the injections.

Following these botox injections, there is generally some bruising around the eyes for about a week. During this time I often accuse my wife of being abusive, but so far no one has believed me!

Meige's Syndrome

Meige's Syndrome is a dystonia that often goes hand-in-hand with blepharospasm. With this dystonia, the muscles of the lower face twitch and move, at times in a rather pronounced manner. In my case, it primarily affects the muscles on the lower left side of my face.

This dystonia becomes most severe when I am driving, when I am tired or under stress, or when I am in bright sunlight. Some of the botox given to me around the eyes has a tendency to "leak" down toward the mouth. For this reason, my teeth never show when I try to smile.

This has a tendency to give my face a somewhat distorted appearance. For the most part, I have little facial expression. When the meige's syndrome is at its worse, it sometimes results in people staring at me and thinking I am mentally retarded.

This is one of the hardest emotions for me to deal with. I have a college degree in Sociology and U.S. History, a Master's degree in Secondary School Administration, and a Master's of Divinity degree. When people observe me at a time when this condition is at its worst, I want to scream out, "I am not mentally retarded!" This is one of the many emotions connected with dystonia that will be dealt with in Part 2 of this book.

You may have noted that I have not included a chapter on the causes of dystonia. This is because we simply do not yet have the answer to this question. We know that dystonia originates within the brain. For this reason, those doctors who have said "it is all in my head" are in reality partially correct! For this reason, I, along with many other patients suffering from dystonia, have agreed to donate our brains to science upon our death. Someday in the future doctors will come to understand the root causes of dystonia and find better treatment options for the disease.

Some evidence points to a genetic abnormality within the brain. Other scientists point to a time of trauma to the brain which manifests itself, often years after the traumatic event. If I had to guess, I believe the second of these hypotheses comes closest to the original cause of my dystonias.

When I was a young boy, I was riding with my Dad on a tractor. He accidentally ran over me when I jumped off the tractor before it came to a complete stop. This resulted in a fractured skull. I recovered and lived a very normal life until my early 40's, the time in which adult dystonias often appear. In my case, spasmodic dysphonia became severe at age 42.

Following my fractured skull, I had a twitch on the lower side of my face and neck in the same area where I now struggle with meige's syndrome. I went to a chiropractor after the accident, and after a couple of months of treatment, the condition went away. I will never know for sure, but this is my best guess as to the cause of my dystonias. Those of us who suffer from this disease look forward to the day in which the definitive causes are known.

Deep Brain Stimulation Surgery

Deep Brain Stimulation surgery is relatively new for dystonia. It has been used for patients with Parkinson's disease for several years with amazing results. Some people with dystonia have achieved significant improvement following the surgery; in other cases the improvement has been minor.

In late January of 2006, my wife made the long drive from Indiana to the Mayo Clinic in Scottsdale, Arizona. We chose to drive because we needed a car while there and were planning to make a trip to Las Vegas to visit our oldest son and his family during the follow-up period in which my Programming Nurse would periodically make adjustments to the settings of my "brain pace-makers". We were fortunate to rent a small house just two miles from the Mayo Clinic.

The Mayo Clinic is a wonderful medical institution. After three days of extensive testing, all of the doctors involved met together to discuss the best course of treatment for me. They concurred that Deep Brain Stimulation might be helpful to my condition.

Prior to doing the surgery, they told me the surgery would not be a "cure" but could result in improvement to some of the symptoms. They explained the risks involved and said that, unlike when using this surgery for Parkinson's disease, they had discovered it would often be eight or nine months before improvement would be seen. As you will later discover, I'm afraid I wasn't listening very well.

At Mayo, they choose to do the surgery in three parts. They feel than an eight-hour surgery where the individual is awake is simply too tiring for the patient. Therefore, they would implant the first electrode, wait a week to implant the second electrode, and then in a third surgery implant the "brain pacemakers" in my chest and run the wires from the electrodes to the pacemaker units, thus completing the process.

The surgery itself is a fascinating experience. My surgeries were scheduled early each morning, and on the drive to the hospital *(the Mayo Clinic and Mayo Hospital are in two different locations)*, my wife and I would play songs by the group Selah: "You Raise Me Up," "Part the Waters, Lord," and "I Need Thee Every Hour." This cd had come as a gift from very special friends in Corydon. These songs, along with the prayers of hundreds of friends back in Indiana, were of great comfort to me.

Upon being called back to the preparation room for my first surgery, they shaved my head and hooked me up to a variety of monitors that would be needed for the four-hour surgery. The first task before going for a final CAT Scan was to attach a "halo" to my skull. These titanium bars that encircled my head would show up on the scan and help provide a "road-map" for the neurosurgeon as he made his way deep into the brain to an area known as the globus pallidus.

While the doctor and surgeon were looking at the results of the CAT scan, I was positioned on the operating table and my head bolted down so it could not move. My programming nurse was constantly by my side, answering any questions I might have during the surgery. The brain is incapable of feeling pain, so for most of the surgery I would be awake. This would help the neurosurgeon to be aware if the electrode was impacting any areas affecting things like sight or other body functions.

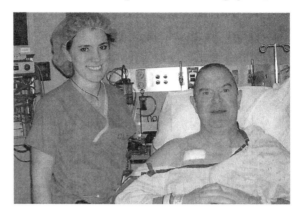

The operation begins with the neurosurgeon drilling a hole about the size of a dime in the skull. Again, the brain feels no pain, so I felt nothing as I heard the sound of the drill at work. However, it is rather un-nerving to realize that just behind a plastic drape a hole is being drilled into your skull.

At this point, the surgeon inserts a very thin wire that allows him to "listen" to the firing of various areas within the brain. Each section of the brain has a distinct firing pattern that can be heard. Throughout this locating process, I was continually asked how I was feeling and to perform certain actions. When the neurosurgeon believed he had found the right location, he replaced the mapping electrode with the thicker stimulating wire and anchored it to the skull with a plastic cup. I was required to stay one night in the hospital following the first two surgeries for observation.

This process was repeated on the other side one week later. Unable to move my head, out of curiosity I asked my programming nurse how many people were in the operating room, as it seemed to be alive with activity. Her answer was, "about 15." This was obviously not routine gall bladder surgery! In fact, I was asked about two months later to pray for a man who had suffered a brain aneurism while undergoing this surgery and was in critical condition. At the end of the first two surgeries, the wires that would be run to my Medtronic pacemaker units were curled up and implanted between the skull and my outer skin.

I would be put to sleep for the final surgery a week later. In this surgery, devices about the size of a silver dollar were implanted into my chest. These would later be turned on to provide the electrical stimulation to the areas deep within the brain that control movement. The two wires were run between the skull and my scalp to the back of my head, around the ears, and into the chest and then connected to the small Medtronic devices.

When I woke up in the recovery room, I felt somewhat groggy. I was glad that at last the process was over. About an hour later, Dr. Evidente came into the room, and to my surprise he suggested that we turn on the pulse generators. This is done by placing a small hand-held device next to the Medtronic devices in my chest cavity and simply pushing the "on" button. I felt nothing, and about 30 minutes later I would return home.

Little did I expect what would happen that evening. My sister had flown out from Indiana to be with Mickey for the final surgery. As the evening wore on, I noticed that all of my dystonia symptoms were disappearing. My voice was reasonably good, and there was no twitching in my eyes. The three of us were ecstatic, feeling that the miracle we had prayed for was taking place right before our eyes. I felt better and better as the evening wore on, and I finally went to sleep wondering if all of this was a dream.

Little did I realize that my long period of "waiting and wondering" was just about to begin.

Waiting and Wondering

I woke up the next morning with a headache. After getting dressed, I soon realized that all of the symptoms that were gone the night before had returned. I was devastated, wondering what was going on. My four hours of sheer bliss had turned into a nightmare!

I went to Renee', my programming nurse, a few days later for my first session of trying to find the best settings for my Medtronic pacemaker devices. She explained that what I had experienced those few hours after coming home from the hospital was a result of the "micro-lesion effect" experienced by some patients following the final DBS surgery. The brain was still in a somewhat swollen condition, masking the dystonia symptoms. As the swelling went down, the symptoms returned.

We began the first of numerous "programming" sessions. This is the hard part of DBS surgery, as there are literally thousands of electrical combinations the nurse can choose from. What Renee' was trying to do was find the "needle in the haystack" that would work for me.

Before returning to Indiana two months later, I probably met with her on about ten occasions. Some settings would cause my foot and leg to twitch uncontrollably. I got very good at staring at the wall across the room as Renee' and Mickey would look at me, trying to find a setting that would calm the twitching motions present in my eyes and lower face. Normally we would find a setting that we thought would work, only to have the results disappear within a few days.

I returned home, wondering if this ordeal had been worth it. During the next two months, I flew twice to Phoenix for follow-up appointments, once again trying to find some settings that would work for me.

During the seven months that followed, I became extremely depressed. Prior to this experience, I had been a fairly social person who enjoyed being around people. Now I didn't want to receive visitors. I didn't want to go out in public. I simply wanted to be left alone. There was constant pain around my neck and in the back of my head. I could find full relief only by sleeping.

I could get some relief by sitting in my chair and reading. I had never been an avid reader, but during those months of waiting and wondering, I must have read 20 books including a complete series of seven novels, each book containing about 300 pages!

One book that was extremely helpful to me was a book by Deborah Farrington entitled The Seasons of a Restless Heart: A Spiritual Companion For Living in Transition. I must have read it at least three times from cover to cover, and I credit it for helping me hold onto some measure of hope in the darkest period of my life. What she was writing about, I was now living.

During this time, I discovered there was a DBS programming nurse at the IU Hospital in Indianapolis. At first, there was little change in my symptoms. But after about nine months of waiting, I began to see some degree of improvement. Carla, my new programming nurse, seemed to have found some settings that were helpful to me, and the constant twitching in my eyes and lower face were starting to become manageable. After about a year I could honestly say that the surgery had been helpful, especially with the blepharospasm and meige's syndrome.

I continue to visit my neurologist and programming nurse at the IU Hospital in Indianapolis approximately every six months for a check-up on my condition. At times we make minor adjustments in the settings of the pacemakers, but for the most part I am relatively satisfied. I am fearful of making major changes, afraid that we will only make matters worse. I am on four milligrams of clonazepam each day. This affects my balance to some degree, but it is helpful with my blepharospasm and meige's syndrome.

The Metronic electrical units are powered by a small battery and must be replaced periodically. Because my settings are fairly high, my nurse called Medtronic when the batteries in my original units were getting low to ask how long new units of the same type would last before having to be replaced again. They estimated approximately 20 months.

Because of this, my original units were replaced with re-chargeable units that will last for ten years. I re-charge them about once a week. This is done by putting sticky tape on a round plastic disk and placing it over the unit in my chest. Attached by a wire to a charging device, it takes about an hour to re-charge each unit.

The replacement was done by simple out-patient surgery. I was at the hospital about three hours total. When I got the bill I almost fainted! The cost was $110,000. Modern medical devices such as these units are not cheap, and I am extremely thankful for the good medical insurance coverage that I have through the United

Methodist Board of Pensions. I laughingly say that they probably hope I die in the not-too-distant future, as my medical bills thus far have far exceeded a million dollars!

I have been asked if I can feel the current that is going from the pulsating units in my chest to the electrodes implanted deep in my brain. At times when I go to bed, if I lay my neck close to a pillow I can feel the continuing pulsation of the electrical current going to my brain. The average person has no idea these devices are a part of my body.

As I close this section of the book, I would summarize my current condition as follows: My voice is poor and it is often difficult for people to understand me, but at least I have some degree of voice. The writer's cramp is well under control. The blepharospasm prevents me from driving and causes me significant problems when in bright sunlight. The meige's syndrome flares up when I am under stress and is often an embarrassment in terms of my facial appearance.

This section has sought to describe each of my four dystonias, their onset, and the efforts of my doctors to treat each one. In the next section I will discuss the far more difficult part of living with dystonia—the ongoing struggle to cope with the wide range of emotions involved.

PART 2

The Emotions Surrounding Dystonia

Papaw Talks Funny

God has blessed us with five grandchildren. Our first grandchild, Gavin, was born premature and died one day after being born from respiratory complications. Our oldest son, Aaron, and his wife, Risa, have two children: Hunter *(age 7)* and Ella *(age 4)*. Our youngest son, Adam, and his wife, Shanna, have two girls: Avery *(age 7)*, and Kayden *(age 5)*. To say they are the joy of our lives is an understatement. It is rewarding to see them so happy and inquisitive; growing up exploring the world around them in ever-new ways each day.

On one occasion a few years ago *(I can't even recall which two grandkids it was who were talking)*, I heard one of them say to the other, quite innocently, "Papaw talks funny." Kids have a way of speaking the truth in a very straight-forward manner, and the fact was this grandchild's comment was quite accurate. Papaw does talk in a way that is difficult for others to understand.

It bothers me greatly that I cannot communicate as clearly with my grand-kids as I would like. I hope, as they grow older, they will come to respect my determination in attempting to do the best job I can in communicating. Communication is something we take for granted until it is lost.

They told me at Vanderbilt that with my advancing age, the build-up of scar tissue in my larynx, and the re-connecting of nerves in ways they do not understand, has caused my voice to become worse with each passing year. Even my wife has difficulty understanding me at times. To say this is frustrating would be a huge understatement. The ability to communicate is foundational for building relationships. Talking in a room with a lot of background noise is nearly impossible for me. For the most part, I try to avoid these situations due to my inability to enter into conversations with people around me. With adults, I have learned that I must face them directly and try to speak slowly if I am to be understood.

There is a plaque that sits on my dresser and was given to me by a wonderful friend in Corydon when the onset of my spasmodic dysphonia occurred. It quotes a verse from Scripture which says, *"Be still and know that I am God."* I trust, as a result of my condition, I have become wiser and a better listener both with God and with others, as much of my life is filled with the silence of my inner thoughts.

As mentioned in an earlier chapter, those of us who suffer from dystonia are not looking for pity. We simply want people to know about our condition and the emotions connected with this disorder. I greatly appreciate people who ask questions with a sincere desire to learn more about my dystonias. For other people who just want to be nice and seem to be interested, I have learned to have a brief answer for the reason that my speech is poor and that other muscles in my body move at times when I don't want them to.

I recall one time when Adam was in high school and we were going to a golf store to buy him a new pair of golf shoes. The person who waited on us remarked that I sounded as if I had a severe cold. I replied, "Yes, my cold is pretty bad today." Upon leaving the store, Adam said, "Dad, you don't have a cold, you have a voice disorder." I replied that he was correct, but it was far easier to simply answer the clerk's comment in the way in which I did rather than try and explain the true nature of my problem.

If you talk to any person who suffers from spasmodic dysphonia, they will immediately tell you the two things that are most difficult for them to do: 1) talk on the phone, and 2) order in the drive-through line at fast food restaurants. To avoid the frustration, I usually go inside a fast food restaurant rather than use the drive-through line. It takes longer, but this way I can speak directly to the person taking my order. Even then they often need to ask me to repeat myself.

The very worst thing for the person with S.D. is trying to communicate on the telephone. I will do almost anything to avoid talking on the phone. I am so thankful for "caller identification." If it is not a person I know, I usually let the answering machine take a message. Mickey does most of my phone calling for me, as it is just too frustrating to try and continually repeat myself. And should I be transferred to a person from India, the phone call turns out to be a disaster!

However, this frustration is heart-breaking when one of the grandkids or another family member is on the line who you desperately want to talk with. Aware of my difficulty in being understood, I simply keep my conversation to a minimum. The use of e-mails in communication has been a tremendous help to me. One thing I never have to worry about is going over the number of minutes allotted to me each month on my cell phone!

I have still been able to preach 8 to 10 times each year due to the help of my wife. I will write out my sermons, and then we will go back and forth in delivering the message. Using a good microphone helps, and this method of preaching allows me time to rest my voice and drink some water in-between speaking, as some of my medications have a tendency to dry out my mouth. I still love to preach, and I thank my wife for getting "way out of her comfort zone" to allow me to preach in this way. In fact, you will find the sermon we most often deliver, "Dealing With Adversity," in the appendix of this book.

We have been asked by several churches to come back and speak for a second or third time. I laughingly remark the time will come when I get a phone call asking if I have a particular date open on my calendar, only to then be told, "We really don't want you, but could your beautiful wife come and fill the pulpit for us on that date!"

There is a device that is helpful to me when I am asked to teach a class or facilitate a small group known as a "ChatterVox." It uses a head-set microphone and a small speaker that allows my voice to be amplified for a group of up to 20 people. It is also helpful when I am conversing with people who are hard-of-hearing.

When I must try to speak for a long period of time, I will be absolutely exhausted at the end of the day from the simple task of talking. A person at the Vanderbilt Voice Center once told me that speaking required the use of more muscles than nearly any other activity one engages in. My body tells me at the end of a day, when I have spoken more than usual, that this is absolutely true!

Romans 8:28 tells us *"all things work together for good for those who love God and are called according to His purposes."* I often want to argue with God about this, as I would still love the opportunity to be involved in pastoral ministry. However, I know, with my activist personality, I would never have taken the time to write two books if my dystonias had not occurred. The first book relates to pastoral ministry, and this second book deals with dystonia and the emotions surrounding it. I trust that hundreds of people will be helped and encouraged through these two books.

At the end of days that have been extremely difficult and frustrating, I sometimes lay my head on the pillow almost hoping that I don't wake up in the morning. I have no fear of death and although I know I would be missed by numerous people, in many ways it would be easier for Mickey if she did not have to care for so many of my needs.

However, I quickly dismiss those thoughts from my mind, as I don't want to miss watching my four grandkids grow up, as they are a joy like no other. I hope the day will come when they will be able to read this book for themselves and realize their very existence was part of the reason that Papaw kept pressing on despite his many struggles!

If you have the ability to speak clearly and without effort, pause for a moment and give thanks to God for something that seems so natural and easy for you to do. Think of how your relationships with others would be affected if you were unable to communicate with clarity. For those of us who suffer from spasmodic dysphonia, speaking is a daily problem we must confront and deal with as best we can.

Feeling Isolated From the World Around You

One of the most difficult emotions a person with dystonia experiences is a feeling of isolation from the world around them. Because parts of your body are moving in ways you can't control, the natural tendency is to withdraw from other people due to feeling embarrassed or self-conscious.

This emotion is perhaps felt most by people who struggle with generalized dystonia *(where numerous large parts of the body are constantly moving)*, or torticollis *(a very painful dystonia where the person cannot keep their head in a straight and upright position)*. However, it is also a struggle for me as well. My inability to speak clearly or loud enough to be heard, combined with my battle with meige's syndrome which causes my face at times to look distorted, often makes me uncomfortable around other people. In those times, I enjoy solitude.

I enjoy rounds of golf with good friends who understand my dystonias, but I can be thoroughly content playing a round of golf simply by myself. However, I confess that I do lose more golf balls when playing alone as there is no one with me to help me see where my ball lands!

As I mentioned in a previous chapter, I was a fairly social person who enjoyed being around people prior to my dystonias. That has changed in recent years and requires a difficult "balancing act" in terms of the times when I need to choose rather or not I want to be around people. It is easy for a person with dystonia to become something of a "hermit." Therefore, it is important that I force myself to get out and be around people. That is most easily done when I know that most of the people I will be with understand my conditions.

However, there are times when it is important for me to say "no" to social interactions and simply play a round of golf by myself or watch a movie or ball-game at home. When I force myself into situations that do not necessarily require my attendance, I will pay an emotional price, both while at the event and when I return home.

This is even true of situations where people understand and are not bothered by my dystonias. Our family has monthly family dinners. I greatly enjoy their company and the fantastic food. However, these events can drain me of my energies. While there I often cannot enter into much of the conversation taking place because of extensive background noise, as our family is large and there are many young children present. I feel a sense of being disconnected with much of what is taking place. I find it is sometimes best for me to attend for a few hours and then return home to an environment which is more comfortable for me.

In my case, there are so many times when I feel there is something that would be valuable for me to contribute to a conversation, but my spasmodic dysphonia makes it difficult to get those comments interjected into the conversation. I can do this when in the right environment. However, often the things I would like to say simply remain "locked" in the inner world of my mind.

The person who suffers from this illness wants to be asked: "How are you coping with your dystonia?" However, people seldom ask this question, perhaps because they feel they are invading an area of the person's life where they don't belong. However, when one is never asked about how things are going for them emotionally, once again they feel disconnected from the world around them.

I compensate for my difficulty in speaking and my inability to currently be involved in pastoral ministry by writing notes to people who are dealing with illness, are discouraged, or who have lost a loved one. It is my way of communicating that "I care." I have found this to be of great help to others as well as giving myself a sense of purpose.

I have a drawer filled with cards from people expressing their appreciation for my ministry with them in a time of need. I often pull several of these cards out of the drawer and read them when I am discouraged. It serves to remind me I have made a difference in people's lives. A dear friend from Franklin once taught me a valuable lesson when she said to me, "Mike, we don't love you for what you can do for us. We love you for who you are as a person."

It is probably good my voice will never return to what it was before. You wouldn't be able to shut me up if it did! The world of isolation is a difficult place to be, but it can also be a very sacred place. It allows one time alone with their inner thoughts and with God, a place where many people who can talk freely never allow themselves to go. With dystonia, always remember that inside every dark cloud one can find a silver lining if they are willing to search hard enough.

Be honest with yourself. Don't allow yourself to become a hermit. Force yourself, when you feel comfortable and safe, to get out and be around people. But at the same time, when you feel the need to withdraw, don't feel guilty when others around you do not understand your need for solitude. The quote, "To thy own self be true," contains profound truth.

There is a song, written by John G. Elliott, which during my nine months of waiting and wondering that followed my DBS surgery, I would play to help me go to sleep each night. I close this chapter with some of the words from this song.

> In this restless world, my heart yearns for a place,
> Where I can go to be with Thee;
> **renewed in peace** . . . . **refreshed through praise**.

> In the quiet of the evening, I will worship you my Lord.
> In the quiet of the evening, I will sing your praise.
> When the day is through, I long to be with You;
> **In the quiet of Your presence**, my Lord.

Depression and Dystonia

Depression and dystonia walk hand in hand. How could it be otherwise when you live in a body which is not cooperating with what you would like for it to be doing? It is nothing to be ashamed of to be taking an anti-depressive medication to help you cope with the many days when you are feeling down and discouraged.

Depression is one of the most common and treatable illnesses in our country today. Sometimes the root cause is chemical in nature. At other times it is brought on by circumstances that have occurred to us in life. I am not at all ashamed to say that I have been on anti-depressive medication for more than 20 years. It has helped to keep my emotions relatively stable as I battle this frustrating illness.

There are moments, even when battling my dystonias, that I have experienced extreme happiness and joy. In fact, I hope I am the kind of person who is constantly looking around the corner for things that bring joy to my life. There have been other times when I have explored the depths of discouragement, unanswered questions, and despair.

Stress does not cause dystonia, but stressful situations may cause one's symptoms to worsen. It is impossible to have dystonia and not experience stressful situations. Since sitting down to work on this chapter, I have received four phone calls. I am expecting a call from a person who lives in another state. Mickey is gone, and so I have picked up the phone to answer each call.

In each of the four phone calls the person calling hung up on me upon hearing the sound of my voice. My attitude was, "that's their problem, not mine." I am actually a fairly nice person to converse with if the other person is willing to work with me and my voice problems!

If asking the question, which came first, the stress or the dystonia, it is kind of like asking the proverbial question, "Which came first, the chicken or the egg?" For the person dealing with dystonia, it is like a cat chasing after its own tail!

There are many different kinds of anti-depression medication. All of them take time for the person to realize that "I am feeling better than I did several weeks ago." Many of these medications are found in a generic version. If one medication doesn't work for you or leads to unpleasant side-effects, consult with your doctor and try another type of medication.

I expect to remain on anti-depression medication until I die. The reason is simple: the medicine is helpful to me. Some people who are very sensitive to medication or are on other drugs where anti-depressive medication might result in complications should consult with their doctor.

To be on anti-depressive medication does not mean you are psychotic in nature. You were probably already told that when searching for a diagnosis! We aren't afraid to take medication if we have high blood pressure. Why then should we be fearful of taking a medication that can significantly help us in battling an illness that produces such highs and lows in our outlook on life?

If you have not tried an anti-depressive medication because of the stigma that was formerly attached to such drugs, my simple advice is to "get over it!" For the most part, I believe this stigma has been greatly reduced in our society. Make an appointment with your doctor and find a medication that is helpful to you.

This is an illness that we will battle every day for the rest of our lives. From my perspective, we need all the help we can get!

Why Am I So Tired?

The person struggling with dystonia often asks themselves this question: "Why am I so tired?" Although I have no formal medical training, I will attempt an answer to this question in this brief chapter.

From the moment you get up in the morning until the time you go to bed at night, your body is fighting against itself. Without realizing it, you are trying to block an activity that wants to naturally occur on its own. On most days, it is our body that walks out of the ring as the victor.

In my case, it requires great effort to speak. To the person with torticollis, it requires great effort to keep their head straight and upright. And to the people who struggle with the most severe dystonia of all, generalized dystonia, they are in a constant battle with the large muscles of their legs, arms, and torso to try and keep them from moving inappropriately.

Some of the medications that we take for dystonia can cause drowsiness. It is often difficult with certain dystonias to get the exercise that our body needs. However, we must work to overcome this obstacle, as I have found that exercise can often lessen the effects of my dystonias—especially if my golf score is good! The combination of all of these things causes us to become more tired than the average individual. It is simply dealing with the reality of living with dystonia.

There is one other factor at work. When we are asleep, most of our dystonias cease. If our dreams are pleasant ones, it is a time that our bodies can be at complete peace. Our struggles begin when we wake up in the morning. Therefore, don't feel guilty if you are tired and want to go to bed at 8 or 9 in the evening. It is simply a fact of life for people with dystonia.

Choosing How We Deal With Our Feelings

There is one lesson in ministry, and also when struggling with dystonia, that I have learned and tried to help people realize. It is this liberating truth: "Feelings are just feelings." It is what we choose to do with these feelings that determines whether we become bitter or become better.

People seem to want to sort out their feelings as good or bad. Anger is often seen as a bad feeling. Joy is classified as a good feeling. I believe our feelings are rather neutral in nature. How we choose to act upon them is what makes all the difference.

The key word here is attitude. Chuck Swindoll, a well-known pastor, is quoted as saying, "life is 5 percent what happens to us and 95 percent what we allow to happen in us."

In the award-winning dvd, "Twisted," *(which I refer to in the appendix of this book)*, the lady that is affected by generalized dystonia and also a dystonia that severely affects her speech, is a remarkable example of the virtues of a positive attitude. She finds love in her life and gets married, and she lives each day with an infectious amount of joy. She was truly an inspiration to all of us who suffer from dystonia before her death a couple of years ago.

As this section of the book tries to point out, dystonia results in many different feelings in each one of us. Many of those feelings are very difficult for us to deal with. We all find ourselves with periods of loneliness and discouragement when we wonder if life is really worth living. These kind of feelings are to be expected when dealing with everything that is involved in trying to cope on a daily basis with dystonia. The reality is that life for us is harder than for most people.

We can get help from doctors and medications that assist us in dealing with the symptoms. However, the reality is that for the vast majority of us, we will live with this disorder every single moment of each remaining day that we are alive on this earth.

I try to deal with these feelings in a positive manner, but I often fall far short in my effort. I will sometimes remark to my wife, "I am going into the bedroom for a couple of hours and have a pity-party. I deserve it. But in a couple of hours I will return and we'll get on with the affairs of the day."

Perfection in dealing with the wide range of feelings involved in dystonia is not the goal. Learning to deal with them as best we can is what we should strive for. Our attitude in facing our dystonia head-on is the thing that makes all the difference. Life is not always fair. I cannot change the hand I have been dealt in life. Will I learn, often slowly and with numerous mistakes along the way, to play the hand I have been dealt as best I can, or will I simply "fold" and quit the game? The words, "life is what we choose to make it," are so very true.

It is important that we surround ourselves with positive-minded people. Negative people tend to pull us down. Positive people have the God-given ability to build us up. I have found that participating in a dystonia support group can be very helpful. It serves to remind me that I am not alone, and it provides me with a variety of coping skills which can be helpful to me. My faith has also been a major asset in living a rich and full life, even with the difficult hand that has been dealt to me.

People with dystonia often observe other people whose situation is much worse than what they are dealing with. That may be true and can be helpful in allowing us to maintain a healthy perspective in our life. However, I caution people that while they can find individuals much worse off than they are, this does absolutely nothing to help them as they try to cope with their own situation! Meeting our own challenges in a positive way is entirely up to us.

As I said earlier, as we face this difficult foe called dystonia, we can get bitter or we can get better. I can *"curse God and die,"* as Job's wife in the Old Testament story encouraged him to do, or I can respond to it as Job did by saying, *"shall we indeed accept good from God and not accept adversity?"* However, I do not believe that God causes our afflictions, as you will discover in the sermon contained in the appendix of this book. Will I throw in the towel, or share it with someone else in need? When I am handed a lemon, will I learn to make lemonade?

We need to learn the lesson that Martina McBride taught us in her best-selling country song: "I Never Promised You a Rose Garden." The words of the first verse are as follows: "I beg your pardon, I never promised you a rose garden. Along with the sunshine, there's got to be a little rain sometime."

The answer to dealing with the soaking rains that come our way in life resides within the soul of each one of us. My prayer is that you will have an "in-spite-of" kind of faith that reaches for the many joys life holds for you, while using the thorns of your life to be of help to others along the way.

Realistic Expectations

As we journey through life with this strange illness called dystonia, it is important that our expectations be realistic. When they are not, we only set ourselves up for greater disappointment.

For example, it is unrealistic that I will ever be asked to give the keynote address at some major conference. The person struggling with torticollis will always have difficulty when asked to "hold still" while someone is taking their picture. The person with generalized dystonia will never win a 100 yard dash. In fact, they will be doing well simply to be able to walk. The sooner we learn to accept the reality that certain tasks we performed with ease before our dystonia are now very difficult for us to accomplish, the easier it will become for us to deal with them.

When going to the Vanderbilt Voice Center, before an injection the speech pathologist would ask me questions about how well my voice had done since my last botox shot and how long I had a normal voice. After about ten years, my standard answer to that question was, "It has been so long since I had a normal voice that I have forgotten what it sounds like." Sometimes we can make real progress forward when we learn to forget *what was* and learn to focus on the reality of *what is*.

Realistic expectations not only involve an honest recognition of our current condition, but it also involves an ability to surrender our pride and not feel embarrassed when we struggle to accomplish a simple task. This is hard for us to do, but I have learned that the majority of people are far more understanding and accommodating of my struggle to speak than I am. And those people who would laugh at our struggles and don't want to understand aren't really worth being concerned about anyway!

Having realistic expectations also offers us help in making decisions. There are many things that I would like to do, but having realistic expectations helps me to learn to say "no" which leads to a much healthier and happier life.

Be realistic with your expectations. Learn the liberating power of learning how to laugh at yourself. In my case, although it may not be anything even close to perfect, I still have the ability to speak and, in most cases, be understood. Realistic expectations can be a liberating force in our battle to cope with the feelings involved in living with dystonia.

No Looking Back

Our natural tendency in life is to play the "what if" game and look backwards regarding decisions we have made. The problem is it does us absolutely no good, and in fact causes us to deal with more regrets in life than are necessary, taking from us energies that are needed to face the challenges of today.

The fact is there is absolutely nothing we can do about yesterday; all we are really promised is today; and the future is in God's hands, not ours. Reality tells us we made the best decisions we could at the time in conjunction with input from our doctors.

Having said that, allow me to play back a few of the "what if" games from my own journey with dystonia. But I promise you, as soon as I finish writing this chapter, I intend to forget what I wrote and get on about the business of living today as best I can.

I could think "what if" I had chosen not to have the nerve avulsion surgery. Because this decision resulted in two additional surgeries in the next 11 months, it created a large amount of scar tissue being formed which is complicating my situation today. Perhaps it would have been better if I had simply chosen to leave things as they were.

The reality was, at the time I chose to do the surgery, I was getting only five or six weeks between injections. This pattern had gone on for three years, and I was still involved in full-time ministry. The time and expense in making so many trips to Nashville played heavily into my decision. And the fact is, following the two follow-up surgeries, I was able to remain in ministry for 15 more years.

The fourth experimental surgery, to replace some of the the vocal chord tissue with fat, would be perhaps the decision I would second guess the most if I allowed myself that luxury. The surgery did help my voice to a degree, but the blepharospam and all its future complications came on immediately after this surgery. However, Dr. Netterville was emphatic that there should have been absolutely no correlation between the two events. The blepharospam might have come on anyway, even if I had chosen not to have this surgery.

Second guessing ourselves is as natural as breathing. However, it only results in coming to the dead-end road of unanswerable questions. As much as possible, avoid traveling this dangerous highway. You did the best you could with the information you had at the time. You have more than enough to deal with today without playing the "what if" game.

Finances: A Very Real Issue

I have been among the lucky ones in terms of the very real issue of finances that confront people battling dystonia. I have very good insurance through the United Methodist Church that has covered the majority of my expenses. Although my income has been significantly less during these years of being on disability, the Board of Pensions has provided us an income that has enabled us to meet our basic living expenses.

Where we have gotten hurt is related to our retirement. I will be forced to retire on July 1, 2014. At that point my disability check stops and my pension begins. There have been a couple of times when we were forced to take funds from our pension account in order to meet basic living expenses. All of this has occurred at a time when I should have been able to invest significant funds into my retirement account. I hope to be able to work part-time following retirement *(I cannot work now without my disability income being reduced)*, but finding a job for a pastor who has difficulty in speaking and cannot drive will be a challenge!

However, that challenge pales in comparison to the devastating effects that many people with this disorder face. I have talked with people who had no health insurance or who lost their insurance when they had to stop working. Social security disability helps, but in no way does it cover their basic living expenses plus the high cost of botox treatments. In fact, I find myself rather upset that the cost of botox went up significantly when it began to be used for cosmetic purposes to satisfy the vanity of people who want to avoid a few wrinkles.

Allow me a brief moment to share a humorous story in the midst of this very serious chapter. After my first botox injections for blepharospasm, I had at least four ladies who, upon greeting me after the worship service the following Sunday, remarked that I looked younger. I thanked them for the compliment, but it was all I could do to keep from saying: "Lady, it's the botox!"

When botox began to be used for cosmetic purposes, many of us had to fight with our insurance company to help them understand that we were receiving injections out of medical necessity and not for the purpose of removing wrinkles. In our case, we certainly were not going to "botox parties!"

People with dystonia want to be able to continue their present job, but the effects of their condition often prevent them from doing so. People like me who have difficulty in speaking often find themselves immediately rejected when the potential employer hears their voice on the phone or in an interview.

I really have no answers for people struggling financially due to no fault of their own but rather the onset of their dystonia. My heart goes out to you, as this is a very serious issue for thousands of people dealing with this condition. Seek help from every social agency you can. Be willing to take assistance from churches, individuals, and family members when it is offered.

For many of you, you are fighting one battle with your dystonia and another battle with your finances. It is not a pleasant place for anyone to find themselves.

Giving Up What I Loved to Do

From an emotional standpoint, by far the hardest thing for me to do was to give up a profession I dearly loved. A person often finds much of their sense of identity in what they do. I loved being involved in pastoral ministry. All three of the churches I had served had grown by almost 50 percent. We added new facilities and did remodeling in the last two churches I served, and the churches I pastored were heavily involved in missions.

I loved the people of the churches I was fortunate to serve, and they in turn loved me back. What a privilege it is to be invited to share in the most sacred moments of people's lives: baptisms, weddings, times of crisis, retirements, significant wedding anniversaries, funerals, and the list could go on and on. It is those special times with people that I miss the most.

At the time that my last two dystonias came on, I was pastoring one of the 25 largest United Methodist churches in the state of Indiana. I would have been happy to

have remained there until retirement, but I had attended numerous conferences to prepare myself in the areas of church growth and how to better reach out to unchurched and nominally-churched individuals.

Since leaving the ministry, I have seen many large churches and administrative positions within our Indiana Annual Conference be filled by others and wondered if my dystonias had not come about, would I have been considered for one of those positions? The answer is probably "yes," but it is one of those things that is best not to reflect upon.

When I asked the Bishop for a disability leave in order to go to Mayo for DBS surgery in 2006, there were many people in my church who wanted me to take a temporary leave of absence with the possibility of returning. I met with a retired Bishop and another pastor whose opinions I respected greatly to ask for their advice.

Their answer was simple and correct as they replied, "Mike, it is best for you not to do that. It is not the best thing for the church to be without a key leader, and neither is it the best choice for you. If you took that route, you would constantly be worrying about things back at the church. Now is the time for you to focus on your health and your own well-being." I am so thankful I took their advice, as there was no way I could have returned. It was one of those times when I had the chance to learn the valuable lesson that none of us are irreplaceable.

I am thankful for those pastors who have allowed me to preach in their churches, lead workshops, or teach short-term classes. This has enabled me to stay in ministry in a limited way. Their confidence and support, along with the prayers of dozens of other pastors, has meant more to me than they will ever know. I am also thankful to Bishop Mike Coyner for his appreciation of my ministry and his genuine concern for my well-being.

The writing of two books has proven to be a source of great blessing to me. It has allowed me an outlet for my creative skills, and I trust it has provided help for pastors in their ministry and, in this book, for persons dealing with dystonia and other forms of adversity. I do not in any way consider myself to be an accomplished author, but the feed-back I have received from numerous people who have been helped by these two books has reminded me there are many ways to make a difference in the lives of others.

I want to close this section on the feelings and emotions connected with dystonia with the words of the Apostle Paul. He tells us *"to be thankful in all things,"* and that *"God's strength is often best revealed in our weaknesses."*

Dystonia has certainly caused a disruption in my plans and is a sourse of constant frustration. In no way do I like the situation in which I currently find myself. However, there is a certain sense in which I can say "thank you" for the dystonias that have been a part of my life for the past 22 years. Because of them, I have learned to have more empathy for others going through difficult times of life. It has certainly played a role in the formation of my character. It has given me a greater love and appreciation for my family and friends. It has taught me about the things in life that truly matter.

It has given me a sense of humility that I could have learned in no other way. And finally, it has resulted in a deeper faith and trust in the sufficiency of my Lord and Savior, Jesus Christ, and the hope that His grace and provision are sufficient for my every need.

I close this section of the book with the words of a favorite hymn of mine, "Great Is Thy Faithfulness."

Great is Thy faithfulness, O God my Father.
There is no shadow of turning with Thee.
Thou changest not, Thy compassions they fail not;
As Thou hast been, Thou forever wilt be.

Pardon for sin, and a peace that endureth,
Thine own dear presence to cheer and to guide.
Strength for today, and bright hope for tomorrow,
Blessings all mine, with ten thousand beside!

Great is Thy faithfulness! Great is Thy faithfulness!
Morning by morning new mercies I see.
All I have needed Thy hand has provided;
Great is Thy faithfulness, Lord unto me.

PART 3

Looking to the Future

Finding a New Sense of Normal

When I was in the ministry and members of a family had lost a very significant loved one, I was careful to make two important points at the funeral. I would first say that "with time and the help of God, family, and friends, they would find the strength to go on." But then I would make an equally important second point. Despite what others might tell them, their lives would never again be the same. How could it be, having lost a loved one who had shared life so intimately with them? I pointed out the task now before them was to discover "a new sense of normal."

The same dynamic is present with dystonia. Dystonia also involves a sense of loss. Once its frustrations, emotions, and limitations have fully sunk in to the fabric of our being, the challenge before us is also to find a new sense of normal. Our lives have been forever altered.

Unfortunately, there are some people who are unable to do this. For the remainder of their lives they wallow in self-pity and find every day a burden. Some people even take their own lives, feeling that life is no longer worth living. I can relate to how those people may feel, but that only makes life more difficult for close family and friends as they are constantly left to live with the question of "why?"

Dystonia makes life very hard. There are times when its effects seem overwhelming. One day we feel like we are doing fairly well, and the next day can turn out to be almost unbearable. However, life is what we choose to make it. There are many joys still ahead of us. There is a sense of accomplishment simply in carrying on despite this awful disorder that has radically re-ordered our lives.

We as human beings have the amazing ability to adapt. Yes, our lives will never be the same, but we can go on with purpose and joy in our lives. This new life is discovered only with time and the support of those around us, but we can find a "new sense of normal."

Each individual's "new sense of normal" will be different, depending on their unique circumstances. Allow me to discuss briefly what my new sense of normal looks like.

Without question, my life now is experienced in profound ways through my grandchildren. What a joy it is when we learn to look at life through their innocent and inquisitive eyes. I love the joy found in being around them.

I am less social than before my voice dystonia. However, I find e-mail to be a wonderful way of staying in touch with friends. I still enjoy being involved in ministry in a limited way, and I find the ministry of "listening" to be so much greater than it was before.

As you have no doubt noticed, I greatly enjoy playing golf. The rounds with my two boys and other good friends are a source of tremendous satisfaction to me. Right now, the dystonias have almost no effect on my golf game. I give thanks to God each day for this precious gift. The time may come when I am no longer able to play, and then I will have to find another "new sense of  normal." Finding a new pattern for our lives is not a one-time process. It continues as the normal effects of aging set in.

I value my wife more than ever before, even though I have the awful habit of trying to talk to her with my face looking in the opposite direction *(not a good habit for a person with spasmodic dysphonia and a source of great frustration to her)*. Although our times of communication are less than before, our love for each other has only grown stronger. My physical struggles have caused me to develop a greater appreciation for the pain she lives with on a daily basis. I often tell her, "Please do not die before me. My trade-in value has become very low!"

I have come to value solitude. I find that I do more reading than I did previously. My ability with words, a gift from God, although not spoken nearly as often as before, have found expression in the two books I have been able to write.

My hope is to find some form of part-time employment upon my retirement. However, I have found it is of no value to run ahead of ourselves, as the cares of today are enough to deal with.

We still greatly enjoy traveling. Although our income in retirement will not be what we had planned for, we have come to realize how blessed we are in comparison to so many other people, both in this country and throughout the world.

That is something of what my "new sense of normal" looks like. My life in a sense is slower than it was before, but like other people in retirement, I find my days are usually very full to the point where I often ask myself, "How in the world did I find time to work?"

But in the next chapter, I will discuss the extreme importance of living one day at a time.

Living One Day at a Time

Living one day at a time is so critical in battling dystonia, but it is also extremely difficult to do. It is natural for us to wonder what is coming next. But as Jesus said, *"Today's troubles are all you can handle. Take care of those as they come. God will help you deal with tomorrow's trials when they arise."*

But how much easier this phrase, "live one day at a time," is to say than it is to actually do. As I have mentioned earlier, due to my dystonias, one of the areas I find myself worrying about is whether we will have enough money to last us in retirement. My wife could tell you that I have spent dozens of hours sitting at my desk wrestling with this issue.

The problem with this way of thinking is that tomorrow has not yet been given to us. Yes, it is good and necessary to do careful planning, but when we waste energy worrying about something that has not yet come to be, it only takes away from us the energy that is needed for the tasks of today. This is such a critical lesson for us to learn if we are to rise above our struggles, frustrations, and pain.

The other issue that I deal with is to realize that I will be going to doctors for botox injections for the rest of my life. This is not a comforting thought. Although my doctors have become like family to me, I am starting to hate the ongoing cycle of going for another doctor's appointment. With every doctor visit, it seems like the walls of their offices press in upon me more and more. However, this thought is far too depressing to allow me to go there mentally more than on rare occasions! It is best simply to look at the calendar, see what doctor appointments are on the agenda for the month, and then try to go with a smile on your face!

Again, I have tried to stress the difficulty of living one day at a time. Be aware that in this area, there are bound to be times when you will fail miserably. However, it is the only path that leads to inner peace. Two things have been helpful to me. One is found in my life verses in the Book of Proverbs, chapter 3, verses 5 and 6. They tell us to *"trust in the Lord with all our hearts, and lean not to our own understanding. In all our ways acknowledge Him, and He shall direct our paths."*

When I look back, I have found that God has always proven to be faithful in providing strength, guidance, and provision for my needs; often in very unexpected ways. But I also realize the truth that rarely are these things provided in advance. They are given only as the needs arise!

The second thing I have found helpful in dealing with this essential truth is to ask myself the simple question, "Is the cup of my life half-full or half-empty?" Our answer to this question makes all the difference in terms of whether or not we will rise above the struggles brought on by our dystonias.

I choose to believe the cup of my life is still at least half-full. On my better days, I trust God with the future, accepting the reality that the future has not yet arrived. Despite the constant struggles, I also realize that there are many joys to be found today if only I will look for them.

Believe me when I say this chapter has been written by a "fellow struggler" who probably gets no better grade than a B- in this area of living one day at a time. My prayer for you is that you can learn to live out this invaluable truth, at least most of the time!

Free at Last!

Although I am a pastor, I have tried not to be "preachy" in the writing of this book. I hope you feel I have succeeded in this effort. However, this final chapter is very much written from the perspective of my faith.

Rick Warren perhaps put it best in this quote from his best-selling book, The Purpose Driven Life. He states, "God is more interested in our character than in our comfort." And it is on the anvil of adversity that character is most often hammered out.

I do not believe that God has brought on my dystonias. The reason He has allowed them will be shrouded in mystery in this life. However, because of the life, death, and resurrection of Jesus Christ, I believe with all my heart that I will someday enter into His eternal kingdom where dystonias, cancer, heart disease, accidents, and all the other trials of this life will no longer exist. In that moment, in the light of eternity, the struggles of this life will be but a fleeting moment in time.

I enjoy all of the benefits that have been mine in this life, even despite the dystonias. I tried to point this out in the very first chapter of this book. But for me, death will be a time of liberation. None of us know how many years on this earth God plans to give us. We are simply called to live them out with the guidance and help of God's

Holy Spirit as best we can. He knows our weaknesses and mistakes, and God has covered them with His marvelous grace.

But when that moment of death comes, I hope to hear these wonderful words from my Savior, *"Well done, good and faithful servant."* In that moment, the bonds of dystonia will no longer hold sway over this earthly body. I will be **free at last!**

I close the book with some of the words of this poem that speaks to the unanswerable questions of life so well. It is entitled, "The Weaving."

My life is but a weaving, between my Lord and me;
I cannot choose the colors; He worketh steadily.
Oft times He weaveth sorrow, and I in foolish pride;
forget He sees the upper, and I the lower side.

Not til the loom is silent, and the shuttles cease to fly;
shall God unroll the canvas, and explain the reason why.
The dark threads are as needful, in the Weaver's skillful hand;
as the threads of gold and silver, in the pattern He has planned.

APPENDIX

Dystonia 101

*Below is a re-print of an article included in "Dystonia Dialogue",
a magazine published three times per year by the
National Dystonia Foundation.*

**Dystonia can be a confusing disorder to understand. It
never hurts to brush up on the basics:**

Dystonia is a neurological disorder. It affects the nervous
system's ability to control voluntary muscle movements.

Dystonia does not affect smooth muscles, such as the heart.

There are many forms of dystonia. It can affect a single body
area or multiple muscle groups.

Dystonia can exist on its own, or be a symptom of another
neurological or metabolic disorder.

In *primary dystonia*, the affected person has no other
neurological symptoms and the dystonia is known or suspected to
be genetic.

In *secondary dystonia*, the symptoms can be attributed to an insult to the brain such as physical trauma, drug-exposure, or other diseases or conditions.

People with secondary dystonia often have other neurological symptoms, some of which may affect more than just one muscle movement.

Each case of dystonia is classified by: the age symptoms started, whether it can be classified as primary or secondary, the body parts affected, and the presence or absence of other disorders.

Treatment options include oral medications, botulinum neurotoxin injections, surgery, and less invasive methods such as physical and occupational therapy, and relaxation practices.

While stress does not cause dystonia, symptoms may worsen in stressful conditions.

Suggested Resources

The primary source of information related to dystonia is the National Dystonia Foundation. A variety of information can be found on their website at: www.dystonia-foundation.org

This organization also publishes a wonderful magazine entitled "Dystonia Dialogue" three times each year. This publication contains human interest stories as well as information on the latest in dystonia research.

The documentary film, "Twisted," by Laurel Chiten, won several national awards. It contains stories of people battling generalized dystonia, cervical dystonia, and torticollis, dystonias not discussed in any great detail in this book. It also discusses Deep Brain Stimulation surgery for dystonia and provides invaluable insights related to the emotions involved in battling this disorder. For more information on how to obtain a copy, contact the following website: www.blinddogfilms.com

A wealth of information related to the dystonias discussed in this book can be found using any computer search engine.

For people who have dystonia, the National Dystonia Foundation urges you to donate your brain for scientific research after your death. The Harvard Brain Bank coordinates this important endeavor. There is no expense to the family, and becoming a brain donor has absolutely no impact on funeral arrangements. For more information, you can contact them by phone at 800-377-3978.

I researched several sound amplification units and felt the ChatterVox unit, mentioned in Chapter 10, provided the clearest quality of sound and the most practical size of any of the units I tried. At the time this book was written, the cost was $285. For more information about this unit, contact www.ChatterVox.com

Sermon:
"Dealing With Adversity"

(Romans 5:1-6)

In M. Scott Peck's book, **The Road Less Traveled**, the first line reads as follows, *"Accept the fact that life is hard."* And if we look at most of the characters in Scripture, including our Lord, those words reflect their lives as they sought to follow God.

Almost everyone deals with some form of adversity—something in your life you wish you could change but cannot. Life is filled with pain and adversity, no matter how strong your faith might be.

Now it is true that much of life is filled with numerous blessings. But what are we to do when the storms of life come our way? And they will come. In fact, Jesus in the Upper Room said to His disciples: *"In this world you will have problems."*

Yet one of the most important words in Scripture follows this promise from Jesus. It is the little word "but." The entire passage reads: *"In this world you will have problems, **but** be of good cheer, for I have overcome the world."*

Dealing with adversity has been a reality for me for the past 20+ years. It began in 1992 when I was pastoring Old Capitol United

Methodist Church in Corydon. God was blessing my ministry there, but suddenly my voice went from totally normal to a point where I could barely speak at all.

I was diagnosed as having spasmodic dysphonia, a rare and currently incurable neurological disorder which causes the tiny muscles that control the vocal chords to spasm, making speech very strained and effortful. Soon after this, I developed a second dystonia that affected the muscles in my right hand, making holding a pen and writing almost impossible.

Needless to say, I was scared to death, as being able to speak and write are extremely critical elements to being in ministry!

I began what has now been over 100 trips to the Vanderbilt Voice Center in Tennessee for botox injections and four surgeries. I had to develop a new approach to ministry, but a far more Biblical one, that of "equipping the laity for their ministry." There was a quote that I would often use at that time. "I can no longer play my instrument as I would like, but I can still conduct the orchestra, and an orchestra makes far more beautiful music than a soloist!"

In fact, a wonderful gift was given to me at that time by one of my members. It was an orchestra baton engraved with the verse Ephesians 4:16 which talks about this important role of a pastor.

Over the next 13 years, the churches I served continued to grow and prosper. I was discovering the reality of the sufficiency of God's grace and the truth of the promise in Scripture that *"when we are weak, God is strong."*

But from 2003-2005, I developed two more dystonias, one affecting my eyes making it no longer safe for me to drive, and a fourth dystonia affecting the muscles in my lower face.

Four eye surgeries and botox injections produced only limited results, and in 2006 I had no choice but to go on disability and leave the ministry in the prime of my career.

I traveled to the Mayo Clinic in Arizona for Deep Brain Stimulation surgery. They told me ahead of time that the surgery was not a cure but could improve the symptoms to some degree. That proved to be true, but not to the degree that I could return to full-time ministry.

A book that was very helpful to me in this difficult time was entitled **Seaons of a Restless Heart** by Debra Farrington. In it she writes these words:

"A chronic illness (Debra has M.S.) and any number of other adversities all share one thing in common. They dump us into an unsettled time . . . a restless season . . . a journey that seems like desert space . . . where the horizon seems to stretch on endlessly, leading nowhere."

What I would like to do in this message is to share briefly eight lessons that I have learned as I have dealt with my own adversity in the hope that they can be of help to you in whatever adversity you may find yourself dealing with.

Be careful who you blame.

People often say: *"I think everything happens for a reason."* But ultimately that statement traces the cause of our afflictions back to God. And who would want to serve a God who causes all of life's trials and tragedies?

I don't approve of the wording that is used, but there is real truth in the bumper sticker that many of you have seen that says: "S*** Happens!"

Satan, not God, is the cause of our adversities. But God can use the adversities of life to mature us and make us even stronger in our faith.

In II Corinthians 12, the Apostle Paul writes these words, *"There was given me a thorn in the flesh, an instrument of Satan, to torment me. Three times I pleaded with the Lord to take it away from me. But He said to me, My grace is sufficient for you, for my power is made perfect in weakness."*

Learn to see God's healing in a broader perspective.

Do I believe that God could reach down and take away my illness in an instant? Yes! Miracles still happen every day. And yet there is a sense in which I believe I have received God's healing, even though the dystonias remain.

II Corinthians 4 says: *"But we have this treasure (which is the gospel) in jars of clay to show that the all-surpassing power is from God and not from us. We are hard pressed on every side, but not crushed; perplexed, but not in despair; persecuted, but not abandoned; struck down, but not destroyed.*

Therefore we do not lose heart. Though outwardly we are wasting away, yet inwardly we are being renewed day by day. For our momentary troubles are achieving for us an eternal glory that far outweighs them all. So we fix our eyes not on what is seen, but on what is unseen. For what is seen is temporary, but what is unseen is eternal."

Count your blessings.

My life has been, and remains, incredibly good. No matter what adversities we face, there is so much for which we can be grateful. Rev. Chuck Swindoll says that *"attitude is everything! Life is 10 percent what happens to us and 90 percent what happens in us!"*

And Rick Warren writes: *"In happy moments . . . . **Praise God**. In difficult moments . . . . **Seek God**. In quiet moments . . . . **Worship God**. In painful moments . . . . **Trust God**. And every moment . . . . **Thank God**."*

Allow yourself times of discouragement, anger, and grief.

This lesson is so important. There are times when I get incredibly depressed and discouraged. To not be able to engage in the ministry that I love to do is very hard for me. Sometimes I say to Mickey: "I'm going into the bedroom and have a pity-party for the next hour or so. Then I'll be out and we'll get on with the business of the day!"

Don't let Satan beat you up in those times you feel angry, depressed, and discouraged. Those are normal emotions. Just don't let yourself stay there!

Learn to let go.

We so often believe the lie that, if we just work hard enough, we can be "in control" of life. Adversity quickly teaches us otherwise. In Debra's book I mentioned earlier, she writes:

"In the midst of adversity, sometimes we have to let go of our need to control . . . . to know . . . . and to do everything. We are in unknown territory, trying to find our way to a place we've never been, which doesn't seem to even be on the map! That's exhausting, and just the process of continuing to walk the walk is enough to try and manage."

Accept the love and support of others.

That's easier said than done. It's more fun to be on the giving end. Being angry or blaming others is easier in times of adversity than asking for help.

But what we forget is this: that asking for help is a gift not only to us but to the person who asked as well.

My programming nurse at Mayo said it to me so well one day. Knowing how discouraged I was, she said to me: "***Mike, you are not your illness!*** *You may never be able to return to full-time ministry, but by how you choose to deal with this illness, and by continuing to do what you can, you can still be of great encouragement to others."* I have found her words of wisdom to be so very true.

Never lose your sense of humor.

In the midst of our tears and pain, we must also **take time to laugh.** It truly is the medicine of the soul.

I had a dear friend in Corydon by the name of Susie Evans. Her husband had M.S. He was a big man, and she had to get him up, dress him, feed him, and take care of the majority of his needs throughout the day. In the evening, she would repeat the process as she put him to bed.

In the midst of all of this, I found out that her son-in-law was in jail, charged with arson. Her daughter was in the process of filing for divorce. Realizing all of the stress that she was under, in her yard one day I asked her, "Susie, in the midst of all you are going through, how do you manage to carry on?" She looked me straight in the eye and shared with me one of the greatest lessons I have every learned as she said, "Rev. Mike, you can never, ever lose your sense of humor. If you do, it's over."

Before I move on to my final point, allow me to share this important side-light. We may not want to hear it, but it is so very true. It is a point made by Rick Warren in his best-selling book, ***The Purpose-Driven Life***. It is simply this: *"God is more interested in our character than in our comfort."*

Which leads me to our final lesson.

Learn the lessons God wants to teach you through your adversity.

Rev. Adam Hamilton, pastor of the United Methodist Church of the Resurrection in Kansas City, has a wonderful sermon series entitled, "Lessons From the Farm."

Adam has a large garden which has become a much-loved hobby, and his wife and daughter have two horses. The third sermon in his series has a most unusual title. It is called, "Re-thinking Manure."

In this message, he speaks metaphorically of manure as the illnesses, pain, suffering, and loss that we all go through in life.

He reminds us that manure is not a pleasant thing to deal with. And near the end of his sermon he shares what he had learned about how manure needs to be treated. He discovered that it can't be spread immediately. It needs **time**, such a critical ingredient in dealing with the pain and adversity in our lives. It needs to be turned every seven days until eventually it becomes compost.

In a beautiful analogy, he says that God invites us **every seven days in worship** to bring the pain and suffering in our lives to allow it to be turned by the work of the Holy Spirit until it becomes fertilizer, ready to produce something of beauty as it is spread over the fields of our lives.

That's what our text from Romans 5 is talking about, *"that suffering produces perseverance; and perseverance—character; and character—hope."* And then this promise, *"and hope does not disappoint us, because God has poured His love into our hearts by the Holy Spirit."*

I don't remember much of the Greek I learned in Seminary. But I do remember the word for the Holy Spirit. It is the word **paraclete**, which means "the one called alongside to help in our time of need."

In dealing with adversity, sometimes we do nothing and simply need to "be still and know that God is God." At other times, we are pro-active and partner with God through using gifted, professional people who can provide the skill and counsel we need. But what we don't do is to try to "play God" and tell Him what the future should look like.

Allow me one final quote from the book, ***Seasons of a Restless Heart***. Debra writes these profound words: *"The end of the journey turns out to be one that is ultimately <u>not about us</u>. The end of the* *journey turns out to be about <u>enlarging our hearts</u> so that God can dwell more fully in us and then use the adversities of our lives to minister to others."*

I hope these lessons have been helpful to you as you deal with the adversities in your own life. In no way do I feel I have "arrived" in learning and applying all these lessons to my own life, but God continues to be at work within me.

The bottom line is this, "Life may not always be fair, but God is still faithful and His grace is sufficient . . . . all the time!"

John Wesley, the founder of Methodism, penned a difficult prayer for one to pray. But if we learn to pray it with sincerity, it will change our lives. It is called the Wesley Covenant Prayer. Would you pray it with me in closing.

I am no longer my own, but Thine. Put me to what Thou wilt. Rank me with whom Thou wilt.

Put me to doing; put me to suffering. Let me be employed by Thee or laid aside for Thee; exalted for Thee or brought low for Thee.

Let me be full, let me be empty. Let me have all things, let me have nothing. I freely and heartily yield all things to Thy pleasure and disposal.

And now, O glorious and blessed God: Father, Son, and Holy Spirit; Thou art mine and I am Thine. And may the covenant we have made this day on earth, let it be ratified in Heaven. Amen.

CPSIA information can be obtained
at www.ICGtesting.com
Printed in the USA
LVOW12s1815071116
511969LV00001B/359/P

9 781481 765084